Summary of

Who Moved My Cheese?

by Spencer Johnson

Instaread

Please Note

This is key takeaways, analysis & review

Copyright © 2016 by Instaread. All rights reserved worldwide. No part of this publication may be reproduced or transmitted in any form without the prior written consent of the publisher.

Limit of Liability/Disclaimer of Warranty: The publisher and author make no representations or warranties with respect to the accuracy or completeness of these contents and disclaim all warranties such as warranties of fitness for a particular purpose. The author or publisher is not liable for any damages whatsoever. The fact that an individual or organization is referred to in this document as a citation or source of information does not imply that the author or publisher endorses the information that the individual or organization provided. This concise summary is unofficial and is not authorized, approved, licensed, or endorsed by the original book's author or publisher.

Table of Contents

Overview

A group of old school friends meet to catch up. They end up discussing the unexpected, unforeseen changes to their lives and one friend offers to tell a story about adapting to change. The story he tells involves four characters, two mice named Sniff and Scurry, and two "Littlepeople" named Hem and Haw. All of them are in a maze, looking for cheese, which they need to survive. For the "Littlepeople," cheese also has a larger, metaphysical connotation in the sense that it also makes them happy — their Cheese is thus spelled with a capital C.

All of the characters find a Cheese Station and have a plentiful supply of cheese for a period of time. After a while, however, the cheese starts to run out. One day, when it disappears, Sniff and Scurry understand that their situation has changed and they decide to go in search of new cheese. Hem and Haw, on the other hand, stick around the same spot, looking for cheese and hoping it will reappear. While they are arguing about what to do and ranting about the injustice of their situation, Sniff and Scurry succeed in finding another Cheese Station in the maze.

Despite his fears about venturing into the unknown, Haw eventually decides to leave Hem and go in search of new cheese, too. It's a long journey, but he is exhilarated by the search for something new. Along the way, he reflects on his situation and what he has learned about adapting to change. Haw writes these maxims about change along the wall of the maze in the hope that they might encourage Hem. Eventually, Haw finds a new, plentiful Cheese Station. Although he wants to help Hem, he realizes that no one else can make Hem change.

After the story is finished, the friends discuss its relevance to their lives and how they can apply it in personal and professional situations in order to increase their happiness and well-being.

Important People

Spencer Johnson: Johnson is an author, known for the ValueTales series of children's books and for his 1998 bestselling book, *Who Moved My Cheese?* He is also the co-author of a series of management books.

Key Takeaways

1. Change is an inevitable and constant part of life.

2. Anticipating change can help you better handle it when it occurs.

3. Letting go of old ways and habits can help you adapt to change and embrace new opportunities.

4. Visualizing success and happiness can help you focus on what you can gain rather than what you've lost.

5. Fear is immobilizing and can stop you from embracing new opportunities.

6. It can be exhilarating to break out of old ways and begin the search for something new.

7. It's important to stay in touch with areas outside your comfort zone so you know what's happening around you and are ready for changes if and when they occur.

Thank you for purchasing this Instaread book

Download the Instaread mobile app to get unlimited text & audio summaries of bestselling books.

Visit Instaread.co to learn more.

Analysis

Key Takeaway 1

Change is an inevitable and constant part of life.

Analysis

As Haw reflects on the disappearance of the cheese, he recognizes that circumstances are always changing. The cheese didn't just disappear; it was diminishing all along. He sums up this insight with the idea that "the cheese keeps moving."

The ancient Greek philosopher Heraclitus (535 BCE - 475 BCE) famously observed that a person can never put their foot in the same river twice.[1] What he meant by this was that change is a constant feature of the natural world and of living things. A rushing river, in which water flows in a perpetual, moving stream, epitomizes this idea of life's inevitable alterations and transformations. Likewise, the person who steps into the stream cannot be the same from moment to moment, but is constantly evolving, both physically and in more subtle spiritual and psychological ways.

In an existence characterized by impermanence, the only enduring constant people can expect is change itself. This philosophical understanding has obvious applications in everyday life. For instance, a couple's marriage, though it carries the promise of permanence, is constantly evolving and shifting with the changes in each individual and in their ways of relating to each other. In the business world, too, nothing is stagnant. New products, leaders, ideas, consumer interests, and other factors make change an unavoidable feature of the workplace and marketplace.

Key Takeaway 2

Anticipating change can help you better handle it when it occurs.

Analysis

Before the cheese disappears completely, Sniff and Scurry notice that it is diminishing. They expect that it will soon be gone, which helps them prepare for the day when they have to move on in search of new cheese. Because Hem and Haw don't anticipate this change, they are less equipped, emotionally and intellectually, to handle it.

Some changes are unexpected and difficult to really prepare for — a sudden death, for instance, or an unforeseen accident. Many of life's other changes, however, are signaled along the way or even known ahead of time. Parents often struggle, for instance, when their children decide to leave home. It may feel like a sudden break, but parents who anticipate this alteration in their lives plan ahead in order to ease the transition. They take up new activities, or embrace volunteer opportunities. If they worked only part-time or were stay-at-home parents, they might go back to work. These changes require forethought and planning, but by anticipating change, they can ease the feeling of absence that can come with an empty home.

Key Takeaway 3

Letting go of old ways and habits can help you adapt to change and embrace new opportunities.

Analysis

Sniff and Scurry find new cheese a long time before Hem and Haw because they accept the change. By letting go of the old cheese, they are able to discover and enjoy their new cheese sooner.

This idea is best encapsulated in the common maxim that when one door closes another opens. The catch, however, is that if you are preoccupied with the door that has closed — with this loss and the frustration it brings — you might not notice the door that has opened. This is a common experience in the professional world. A market, for instance, may shift away from one product, hurting business and frustrating executives who had expected to profit from certain conditions. As the market shifts, however, there is an opportunity to capitalize on new consumer interests and preferences. The leader who is able to let go of old expectations and adapt quickly to new conditions is more likely to find success than those stuck in the past. For instance, environmental concerns and consumer frustration with gas-guzzling SUVs created a market for more fuel-efficient cars, such as hybrids. Automotive industry leaders who recognized this opportunity have been able to capitalize on the shift. Meanwhile, those who failed to understand the cultural and political change in consumer thinking and its relevance to the car industry missed out on the opportunity.

Key Takeaway 4

Visualizing success and happiness can help you focus on what you can gain rather than what you've lost.

Analysis

Haw periodically visualizes himself discovering and enjoying the new cheese. This mental motivation helps him continue on his search, despite disappointments, and it keeps him looking to the future rather than the past.

Visualization of success is a popular psychological and meditation method for helping people focus on achieving their goals. In sports, for instance, athletes might prepare for an upcoming competition not only through physical training and practice, but also through mental visualization techniques: imagining themselves performing successfully on the field or the court. This emphasis on the future and on a positive outcome helps counteract negative thoughts, like the memory of unsuccessful performances in the past or athletes' fears that they won't be able to achieve their goal. Olympians are known to use visualization and imagery techniques as part of their mental preparation. [2] The popularity of these techniques indicate how much success can depend on emotional and psychological conditions — positive thinking, belief in the future, and an optimistic focus on achievement rather than failure.

Key Takeaway 5

Fear is immobilizing and can stop you from embracing new opportunities.

Analysis

Haw delays searching for new cheese because he dreads venturing into the unknown. This same fear is what holds Hem back. By asking himself what he would do if he weren't afraid, Haw is able to conquer his fear and embrace the chance to look for new cheese.

The fear of taking chances is a recurrent feature of immigrants' journeys and struggles. Think, for instance, of poor Irish farmers during the nineteenth-century potato famine that left many starving and without a basic means to provide for their families. Conditions like this motivated many people to take a chance on a new life in the United States. Though the conditions of this life were mostly unknowable and the risks involved in crossing the Atlantic and starting a new life were considerable, there was often more to gain in this situation than there was to lose. Immigrants who took this journey conquered their fears and embraced the opportunities the United States had to offer. They didn't let fear immobilize them in their old lives and circumstances. In popular culture, the immigrant story is often a success story that teaches this lesson: it's a story of upward struggle rather than stagnation, and of new chances and possibilities for a better life. The Kennedy family is among the most famous examples: the

Kennedys came to the United States from Ireland in 1849 and through education and work eventually became one of the wealthiest and most powerful families in the United States.

Key Takeaway 6

It can be exhilarating to break out of old ways and begin the search for something new.

Analysis

Haw hesitates to venture into the maze. But as he begins his journey, he finds himself enjoying the adventure and the search for new cheese. It's more uplifting to move forward than it is to wait behind in the old, empty Cheese Station.

Stagnation, in addition to being a bad strategy for success, is also quite boring. Even when people live in comfortable conditions with all their needs met, it can be unsatisfying to simply let things stay the same. The struggle to achieve a goal, or to go in search of something new, imbues life with a sense of purpose and meaning. It can even be a kind of adventure. The British poet Alfred, Lord Tennyson famously captured this sentiment in his poem "Ulysses." In the poem, the Greek adventurer Ulysses (or Odysseus) is an old man, home from his adventures abroad. He feels deadened by the stagnation of simply staying put. He craves the journey again, so he can "follow knowledge like a sinking star beyond the utmost bound of human thought." He wishes once more, in the poet's words, "to seek, to strive, to find, and not to yield." As a young man away far from his beloved, he craved the safety and security of home, but now he realizes that he feels most alive when he is moving into the unknown.

Key Takeaway 7

It's important to stay in touch with areas outside your comfort zone so you know what's happening around you and are ready for changes if and when they occur.

Analysis

Even after Haw finds the new Cheese Station, he continues exploring areas outside his new home in order to be prepared to leave when his comfortable new situation is disrupted. He knows better what the outside world looks like and he is more emotionally equipped to venture beyond his Cheese Station, as necessary.

In the modern age of ever-proliferating technologies, industries face constant innovation and disruption. This makes it especially important to educate yourself about new ideas, technologies, and ways of doing business — not only in your immediate line of work but also in other areas that may affect your business. In healthcare, for instance, new technology is changing the way doctors conduct certain surgeries. This means that the techniques and tools that doctors learned to use in medical school and residency training are no longer the only ways of doing things. Treatments may even become obsolete, which in some cases may contribute to the large numbers of patients who do not receive the latest recommended care from their doctors. [3] For this reason, doctors are wise to stay up-to-date and informed on developing technologies and techniques, even those outside their immediate medical specialty. This is where attending conferences, reading medical journals, and continuing self-education play an important role. These activities aren't required for the day-to-day practice of medicine, but they are critical for a doctor's long-term success. By staying in touch with new ideas and practices outside their comfort zone and conventional practices, doctors can be better prepared for the changes technology will bring to their work.

Author's Style

Who Moved My Cheese? resembles a children's story or fable. It is very simple in style and structure: there are only four characters, a clear problem to resolve, and a series of morals and lessons that arise from the characters' struggle to overcome the problem. Though Johnson seems to gear his book toward adult readers who can apply these lessons to personal or professional challenges, he writes in language basic enough for a child to understand. In this regard, the narrative is very thin and even boring for an adult reader. Nonetheless, this pared-down structure offers a compelling, memorable way to explain and deliver Johnson's lessons about adapting to change. These lessons are delivered throughout the story in the form of Hem's writing on the wall of the maze. Johnson also lists the main lessons at the end of the story as a way to emphasize them to the reader.

The fable about cheese is framed by a group of adults discussing their lives and their struggles with life changes. One of them tells the story about the cheese. After he finishes telling it, they all discuss its relevance to their own lives. This framing is contrived and does not add to the lessons imparted by the fable, but is rather intended to encourage readers to apply the fable's lessons to their own lives.

Author's Perspective

Johnson writes to motivate his readers to adopt the lessons and attitudes that the cheese fable teaches. In this regard, it is obvious that he believes the morals of his story can help people improve their lives by learning to anticipate and adapt to change in both their personal and professional lives. He thinks this is something many people struggle with and he aims to help them rethink the way they deal with change.

Thank you for purchasing this Instaread book

Download the Instaread mobile app to get unlimited text & audio summaries of bestselling books.

Visit Instaread.co to learn more.

References

1. Plato, *Cratylus*, 402a.

2. Clarey, Christopher. "Olympians Use Imagery as Mental Training." *The New York Times.* February 22, 2014. Accessed January 11, 2016. http://www.nytimes.com/2014/02/23/sports/olympics/olympians-use-imagery-as-mental-training.html?_r=1

3. Neale, Todd. "How doctors can stay up to date with current medical information." KevinMD.com. *MedPage Today.* December 14, 2009. Accessed January 11, 2016. http://www.kevinmd.com/blog/2009/12/doctors-stay-date-current-medical-information.html

CPSIA information can be obtained
at www.ICGtesting.com
Printed in the USA
LVHW012244080719
623463LV00019B/646

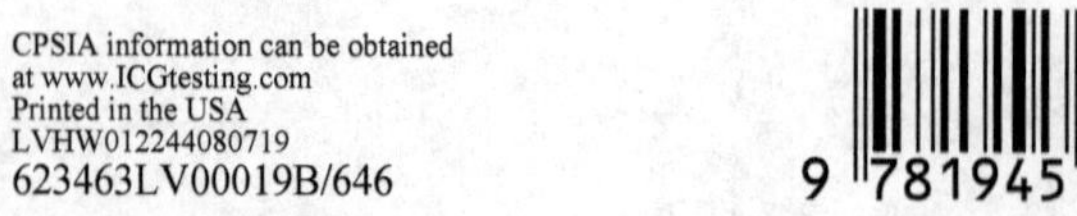